A Guide for Using

The Magic School Bus® in the Time of the Dinosaurs

in the Classroom

Based on the book written by Joanna Cole

*This guide written by **Ruth M.** ~ M.S. Ed*

Teacher Created Materials, Inc.
6421 Industry Way
Westminster, CA 92683
www.teachercreated.com
©1996 Teacher Created Materials, Inc.
Reprinted, 1999
Made in U.S.A.
ISBN 1-57690-087-8

D1531059

Illustrated by
Wendy Chang

Edited by
Walter Kelly, M.A.

Cover Art by
Dianne Birnbaum

Table of Contents

Introduction

The use of good trade books can enhance the study of science. The key to selecting these books is to check them for scientific accuracy and appropriateness for the level of the students. *The Magic School Bus*® series, written by Joanna Cole, contains outstanding examples of books which can help students enjoy and learn about science. These books are delightfully written and scientifically accurate, thanks to the thorough research done by the author as she writes each of her books.

This Science Literature Unit is directly related to *The Magic School Bus*® *in the Time of the Dinosaurs*. The activities in this unit are particularly appropriate for intermediate grades. Teachers who use this unit will find a variety of lessons to do before, during, and after reading the book with their students. These include the following:

- Pre-reading Activity—Identifying dinosaurs and non-dinosaurs
- A Biographical Sketch and Picture of the Author
- A Book Summary
- Activity-oriented lessons which expand the topics covered in the story:
    — hunting for future fossils
    — simulated dinosaur dig with owl pellets
    — constructing a time line of Earth's history
    — mapping dinosaur discovery sites in North America
    — classifying dinosaurs
    — comparing sizes of dinosaurs
    — identifying ages when various species of dinosaurs lived
    — constructing a flipbook of Earth's geologic changes over time
- Post-reading Activity—Inventing an undiscovered dinosaur species
- Unit Assessment
- Annotated List of Books and Materials
- Answer Key

This unit is designed to help you build on the interest your students already have in dinosaurs. The activities will help them develop a better understanding of these fascinating creatures of Earth's past.

Dates of the Earth's geologic history and for the various periods that different species of dinosaurs were on Earth were gleaned from a wide range of resources, all of which are listed in the Resource section. The resources with the most recent copyright dates were used for this information. You may find different dates in recent articles since this information is continuously being revised as new evidence is discovered.

Is This a Dinosaur?

Before you begin reading *The Magic School Bus*® *In the Time of the Dinosaurs* with your students, have them complete the activity on this page which will provide you with baseline data on their knowledge and misunderstandings about dinosaurs. This activity will be used again in the final assessment, so keep the papers for students to compare with their work at the end of the unit.

Ms. Frizzle is about to take her students on another science adventure, this time to study dinosaurs. Before we join her and her students on this trip, check your knowledge about dinosaurs by circling the animals on this page and page five which you think are dinosaurs. If you know the name of the animal, write it in the blank below the picture.

A _____   B _____

C _____   D _____

E _____   F _____

Is This a Dinosaur? *(cont.)*

G _____   H _____

I _____   J _____

K _____   L _____

M_____   N _____

About the Author

Joanna Cole was born on August 11, 1944, in Newark, New York. She attended the University of Massachusetts and Indiana University before receiving her B.A. from the City College of the City University of New York in 1967. She has worked as an elementary school library teacher, a letters correspondent at *Newsweek,* and then became senior editor of books for young readers at Doubleday & Co.

Ms. Cole has written over 20 books for children, most of which are nonfiction. Every writer begins his/her career somewhere; Joanna Cole's began with cockroaches. When she was working as a library teacher in a Brooklyn elementary school, her father gave her an article about cockroaches, describing how they were on Earth before the dinosaurs. She had enjoyed reading science books as a child and remembered finding books about insects to be the most fascinating to her. Since there weren't any books about cockroaches, she decided to write one. Her first book, *Cockroaches,* was published in 1971.

Joanna Cole has written about fleas, dinosaurs, chicks, fish, saber-toothed tigers, frogs, horses, hurricanes, snakes, cars, puppies, insects, and babies, just to name a few examples. Ms. Cole knows that the important thing is to make the book so fascinating that the reader will be eager to go on to the next page.

Teachers and children have praised Ms. Cole's ability to make science interesting and understandable. Her *The Magic School Bus*® series has now made science funny as well. Cole says that before she wrote this series, she had a goal to write good science books told in a story that would be so much fun that readers would read it even without the science.

Readers across the country love *The Magic School Bus*® series and enjoy following the adventures of the wacky science teacher, Ms. Frizzle. Joanna Cole works closely with Bruce Degen, the illustrator for this series, to create fascinating and scientifically accurate books for children. Even a successful writer finds it sometimes scary to begin writing a new book. That was the way Cole felt before beginning to write *The Magic School Bus*® series. She says, "I couldn't work at all. I cleaned out closets, answered letters, went shopping—anything but sit down and write. But eventually I did it, even though I was scared."

Joanna Cole says kids often write their own *The Magic School Bus*® adventures. She suggests they just pick a topic and a place for a field trip. Do a lot of research about the topic. Think of a story line and make it funny. Some kids even like to put their own teachers into their stories.

The Magic School Bus® in the Time of the Dinosaurs

by Joanna Cole

(Scholastic, 1994)

(Canada, Scholastic; UK, Scholastic Ltd; AUS, Ashton Scholastic Party Ltd.)

Ms. Frizzle's students were very excited, Today was Visitors Day at school, and their relatives and friends would be coming to see the exciting displays they had made. They had written dinosaur books, constructed a model of a dinosaur out of chicken bones and clay, and identified some dinosaur models. Ms. Frizzle had other ideas for the day, however. She had received an invitation to visit a real dinosaur dig site, so everyone boarded the old school bus for their next adventure.

When the students arrived at the dig, they met the paleontologist, who had gone to high school with Ms. Frizzle. The students saw people digging out the fossil bones of a duckbilled dinosaur called *Maiasaura*. Once the bones had been chiseled from the rock, they were covered with burlap and wet plaster to protect them from chipping. Later they would be shipped to the museum.

The paleontologist mentioned that he was looking for fossil eggs; this gave Ms. Frizzle an idea. She told the students to get back on the bus. Before they knew what was happening, the bus changed into a time machine and began to go back in time to 225 million years ago. The area, which is a desert today, was then a jungle with early dinosaurs which were small and light. The students observed one of them hunt for food, such as huge dragonflies, small lizards, mammals, and amphibians. Even the plant life was different, with horsetails, ferns, conifers, and gingko trees. A sudden downpour made them race back into the bus.

They moved forward in time to 213 million years ago, when enormous sauropods roamed the area. Suddenly, an allosaurus was seen attacking a wounded stegosaurus, which soon became its dinner. The students and Ms. Frizzle ran back into the time machine and pushed ahead to 144 million years ago. They could see huge flying reptiles and sea reptiles, including turtles, elasmosaurs, and ichthyosaurs. They kept traveling forward in time, finding the weather had cooled, with flowers and fruits everywhere. They saw tyrannosaurs chasing a pack of troodons. The class ran up a hill to escape them and came upon a nesting site of maiasaura mothers feeding their babies. Suddenly, the troodons appeared and began to attack the babies. Without warning, a sandstorm blew up, covering the dinosaurs and nests in a thick layer of sand. The students and Ms. Frizzle made it back to the bus just in time, only to see an asteroid approaching the Earth. Just as it was about to hit the Earth, Ms. Frizzle pushed the forward button, carrying everyone back to the present time.

Back in the classroom, the students made a chart of their trip to share with their visitors. The visitors enjoyed their displays but were puzzled by the realistic videotape of the dinosaurs.

Hunt for Future Fossils

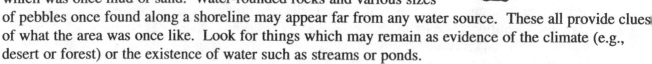

To the Teacher: Even though paleontologists dig up fossils of animals from millions of years ago, fossils continue to be formed. Take the students on a Future Fossils Hunt in a natural area near the school or within easy traveling distance. Preview the field trip site to search for things which may be fossils millions of years from now. These may include fallen feathers, leaves, and trees; animal footprints, skin prints, feces; parts or whole bodies of dead insects or other animals; and animal burrows which could fill with mud. Plants and algae, as well as ripple patterns, have been found in rock which was once mud or sand. Water-rounded rocks and various sizes of pebbles once found along a shoreline may appear far from any water source. These all provide clues of what the area was once like. Look for things which may remain as evidence of the climate (e.g., desert or forest) or the existence of water such as streams or ponds.

Materials: transparency of How Fossils Are Formed (page 9), natural area to search for possible future fossils, plaster of Paris, paper cup and spoon, water, drawing paper and pencil, Future Fossil Hunt data sheet (page 10), cameras (optional)

Procedure: Use a transparency of How Fossils Are Formed (page 9) to explain the process of fossilization. Tell the students that fossils are still being formed today. Explain that the class will be going on a field trip, just as Ms. Frizzle's students do, to search for possible future fossils. Describe the area where they will be doing the hunt. Form groups of three or four students and distribute a copy of the Future Fossil Hunt data sheet to each group. Let each group complete the section to be done before the hunt. Have each group share their ideas from the data sheet before beginning the trip.

On the day of the fossil hunt, take the materials to make plaster casts of any footprints you find. This can be done by mixing plaster of Paris with water in a paper cup until it becomes a runny paste. Pour it carefully over the footprint and then let it dry until it is firm (about 10 minutes). Carefully pull the hardened plaster away; you have made a cast of the reverse print. These are often found in fossil beds, as well as the actual footprints which may have been made in sand or mud which was covered over by more sand or mud, gradually compacting over millions of years.

Have students take their Future Fossil Hunt data sheet to complete during the trip. You may also want to have them photograph or videotape scenes of things they think may become future fossils.

Closure: Discuss the data sheet record each group has completed. Let students place their data sheets in a display area, along with the pictures, video, plaster casts, and actual fossils students may bring from home. Arrange a time to share the displayed items with another class or family members on a Visitor's Day.

How Fossils Are Formed

Fossils are any remains of past ancient plant or animal life. These include imprints of leaves, skin, feathers, or footprints; insects encased in tree sap; and bones or teeth which are replaced by minerals which harden into rock. It is important to realize that most animals and plants do not turn into fossils when they die, but sometimes conditions are just right and their remains are fossilized.

The drawing below shows one way a fossil is formed. A dinosaur drowns as it tries to cross a raging river and is swept toward a sandbank. There it is partially covered by sand and its body begins to decay. Some carnivorous (meat-eating) animals discover it and pull away parts of its body to eat, leaving only a few bones and the skull to be buried by more and more sand. The sand gradually turns to rock, and the bones decay, being replaced by dissolved minerals which eventually harden into rock in the exact shape of the bones. This process takes millions of years.

Erosion of the rock around the fossil bones brings them to the surface again, and some of the bones are discovered by people who are passing by. They take some of the bones to scientists who come to dig out the fossil bones so they can be taken to a museum to be studied and displayed for others to see.

Future Fossil Hunt

Members of this Fossil Hunting Team: _____

_____

Before beginning your fossil hunt, complete the following:

You are paleontologists who are being sent on a mission to examine a natural setting and locate things which might become fossils in the future. List four different types of fossils which have been discovered (e.g., footprints).

1. _____   2. _____

3. _____   4. _____

Now, list what you may find on your hunting trip that could possibly become fossils millions of years from now.

1. _____   2. _____

3. _____   4. _____

During your fossil hunt, complete the following:

Draw two different things you found which could possibly become fossils. Include as many details as possible and label the parts of your drawing.

Describe what would need to happen for these to become fossils:

_____

_____

Most plants and animals which die do not become fossils. What might happen to prevent the things you drew from becoming fossils?

_____

_____

Digging Up Dinosaurs

Usually only a few bones of a dinosaur are preserved as fossils. The paleontologists become detectives, using whatever bones they find as clues to tell what animal they are from, how big it was, and what it ate. Putting the bones together to reconstruct the animal is like assembling a jigsaw puzzle with many missing pieces. The drawing below shows a sketch of the skeleton of the *Baryonyx,* a 30-foot-long dinosaur which lived 120 million years ago. Its fossil was discovered in 1983 in England, and only the white parts of the skeleton were found. Scientists examined each fossil bone carefully to decide where it fit in the body. They were able to fill in the missing parts by knowing what animal skeletons look like today. The missing bones are made from clay or wax. Then a rubber mold is made from these and is filled with resin and glass fibers which harden into the shape of the bones. Fossils and these synthetic bones are then used to reconstruct the skeleton.

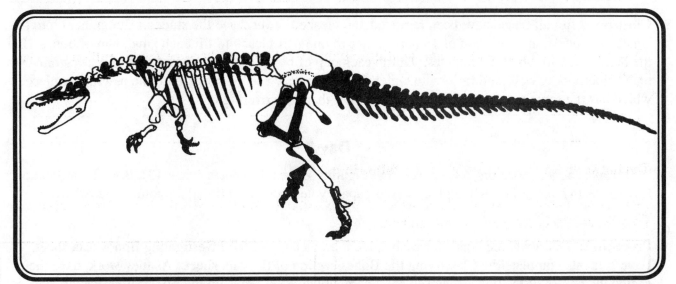

A dinosaur fossil dig site is very much like an owl pellet. Owls are birds of prey which eat rodents, birds, and some insects whole but cannot digest the bones, fur, or hard insect parts. They gather these indigestible parts in their stomachs, and the muscles form them into a ball which the owl spits out. These owl pellets are filled with bones from many animals all jumbled up, rather than containing all the bones from a single animal. Like a fossil bed, they are a treasure chest of bones waiting to be investigated.

Let's dissect owl pellets so we can compare this to digging up and investigating dinosaur fossils.

To the Teacher: This activity will take several hours to do a good job, so it should be spread over at least two days.

Materials: Each pair of students will need one owl pellet, a small cup of water, and a pair of tweezers.

Each student will need a paper towel, 1 oz. (30 mL) plastic cup with a number on it, a piece of newspaper about 5 in. x 5 in. (12.5 x 12.5 cm) with the same number on it as the cup, and a paper towel.

Lesson Preparation: Place the owl pellets in a container and soak them in water for approximately 15 minutes to soften the ball of fur. Number the cups and newspaper pieces, assigning a different number to each student.

Digging Up Dinosaurs (cont.)

Day 1

Procedure: Pair the students and provide each with the materials, except the small piece of numbered newspaper. After covering their work areas with newspaper, students begin by gently pulling the pellets into two parts and giving half to their partners. They feel for bones among the fur, pulling them out and laying them on the paper towel. Tweezers may be used for help. Toothpicks are used to clean fur from areas like the skull and vertebrae. Bones may be dipped in water to loosen fur. As the students work, let them guess what part of the animal (e.g, leg, skull, jaw, etc.) the bone came from. If something unusual is found, such as part of an insect or a bird skull, place it on the overhead projector for all to see. Also, place a paper clip on the projector for a size reference.

Closure: After all bones have been removed and cleaned of fur, have the students dump them into the small cup. Make up a solution of 16 parts water to one part bleach to fill each small cup of bones. Let the bones soak for about 20 minutes. Dump each cup of bones individually into a fine mesh strainer (a tea strainer works well) and rinse with water. Dump out each set of bones onto the newspaper piece which has the same number as the cup and then let them dry overnight.

Day 2

Materials: bones, tweezers, toothpicks, Investigating Bones data sheet (page 13), Bone Identification Key (page 14), magnifier, white glue, waxed paper, Vole Skeleton (printed on colored paper) from page 15.

Procedure: Distribute the bones for each student and a copy of the Investigating Bones data sheet. Have students complete the Classifying the Bones section of the data sheet. As they work, have them decide the names of the bones themselves. Share any unusual items on the overhead projector.

Once most students complete identification and classification of their bones, let them move on to Reconstructing an Animal. Do not offer assistance; it is important that students try this on their own and develop an understanding of what paleontologists do when reconstructing a dinosaur. They may work in groups, however, and offer suggestions to each other, just as scientists do. When most students have completed this section, have them rotate among the work areas to view what other students have done. Discuss what they discovered—e.g., that different sizes of similar bones indicate they are from different animals.

Distribute the identification sheets and have students complete the last part of their data sheets.

Closure: Have students select various bones to glue on the Vole Skeleton, placing them over the actual matching bones. Apply the glue with a toothpick in a thin layer; it will dry clear. For larger items, place a drop of glue on the picture and then lay the bone on top of it. Include extra bones by gluing them alongside the bones drawn around the skeleton. Glue any unusual items (e.g., bird skull, beetle skull) on an empty space and label them. Mount the pictures on cardboard and display them in the room.

Investigating Bones

Classifying the Bones

1. In the box below, sort the bones from your owl pellet by shape and then write in pencil what part of the body you think they came from.

2. Did all of these bones come from one animal? _____ How do you know?

_____

Reconstructing the Animal

3. Use the bones from your Classifying the Bones section to reconstruct the animal(s) they came from. Put the bones where they would have been located inside the body. Can you find any bones together, such as a leg and hip?

4. Use the Bone Identification Key on page 14 and the Vole Skeleton on page 15 to decide what the bones really are. Glue the bones on the Vole Skeleton, matching them with the drawings.

5. Measure the leg bones and then write how tall these animals were. If you found only one leg bone, double it to get the size. How tall were the animals? _____

_____

Bone Identification Key

	Voles and Rats	Mice	Shrews	Birds
Skull and Jaws	Teeth	Tooth	Tooth	No Teeth
Hips (pelvis)				
Shoulder (Scapula)	The shoulder blade is similar in all of these animals.			
Other	Mole Skull and Jaw	Beetle Wings / Insect Leg	Fish Bones / Scales	Bird Breast Bone / Wing Bone

Vole Skeleton

Glue the bones from your owl pellet on the skeleton below, placing them directly over the bones, even if they are larger or smaller. Put the extra bones beside the drawing of the bones around the skeleton. If you found anything other than bones, glue it at one corner of the picture and write what it is. If you have not been able to identify it, write what you think it is, followed by a question mark (?).

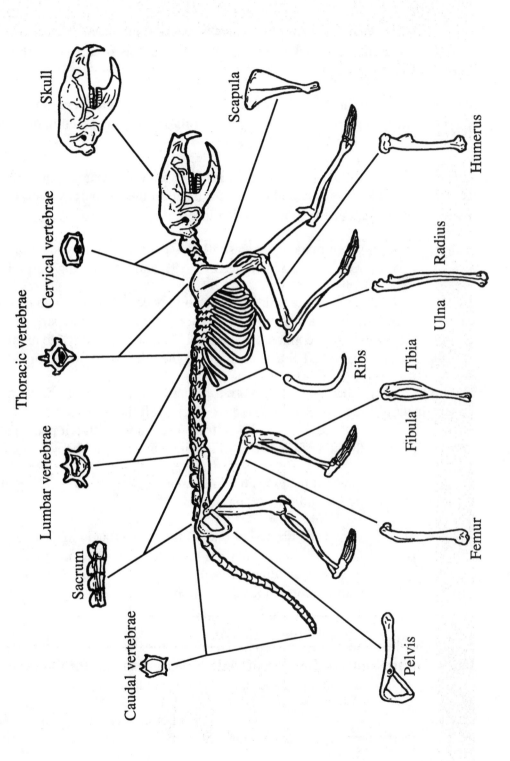

Skull

Scapula

Humerus

Cervical vertebrae

Radius

Ulna

Thoracic vertebrae

Tibia

Ribs

Fibula

Lumbar vertebrae

Femur

Sacrum

Caudal vertebrae

Pelvis

Time Line of Earth's History

After the paleontologists mentioned that they had found fossils of Maiasaur but no nest, Ms. Frizzle rushed all the students onto the bus and drove off a short distance. She stopped the bus and turned a dial on the dashboard. Suddenly, the bus became a giant alarm clock and time machine. The hand on the clock started moving backward, taking the bus and its occupants back 225 million years to the late Triassic Period.

Let's travel through the 4.6 billion year history of our planet by creating a time line. This time line will show the changes on Earth during those billions of years, including plants and animals which evolved and extinctions that took place.

To the Teacher: The data for this time line is based on current scientifically accepted theory. The reference books used to collect this data are listed in the Resources section. (Note the *National Geographic* article on extinction by Rick Gore.)

Materials: pencils, felt markers, at least 50 meters of 3" (8 cm) wide adding machine tape, meter sticks, copy of the Earth Time Line (pages 17–19), and Interpreting Earth Time Line (page 20)

Procedure: Divide the students into groups so they can share the load of making the time line. Distribute a copy of the Earth Time Line to each group. Distribute strips of adding machine tape to each group according to the amount needed for their section. Provide extra length for each strip of tape, which will be trimmed before adding it to the other strips in the time line.

Explain to students that they are to work together to measure their adding machine tape according to the information listed on the time line data sheet. Tell them to use pencil to mark the divisions of each section and record the life forms and then trace over these with felt pen. They will need to leave about 1 inch (2.5 cm) at the end of each strip so it can be attached to the next one.

Students should not record the extinction information until the time line is all linked together. Write this information in red to indicate its importance.

Closure: Help students tape the end of one section to the beginning of the next, starting with the earliest period. Roll the sections as they are taped together to avoid getting them tangled. Once all sections are linked together, the time line will be 46 meters long. Place it on the walls around the classroom or go outside and use clothes pins to hold it to the playground fence. Have each group take turns serving as tour guides through their section of the time line.

Display the time line in the classroom. Distribute the data sheet Interpreting Earth's Time Line to each student and arrange a rotation system so students can examine the time line as they gather their data. They should also have access to the Earth Time Line data.

Extension: Hang the time line around the classroom. Make a copy of the *Magic Bus*® Time Machine and place on the time line. Move it along through the various periods as this unit progresses.

Earth's Time Line

(Scale: 1 meter = 100 million years ✧ 1 centimeter = 1 million years)

CENOZOIC ERA

Period	Millions of Years Ago	Examples of Life Forms	Length of section
Quaternary	0–2	Modern humans begin to develop into what they are today.	2 cm
	4	Australopithecus, closest primate ancestor to humans, appears in Africa.	2 cm
	10	Ramapithecus, oldest known primate with human-like traits, evolved in India and Africa.	6 cm
Tertiary	40	Monkeys and apes evolve. Camels, cats, dogs, elephants, horses, rodents, and huge rhinoceros-like mammals developed.	30 cm

Extinction at the End of the Cretaceous Period

Many marine species are killed and the dinosaur era ends. Scientists believe the cause may have been from an asteroid or comet striking the Earth.

Earth's Time Line *(cont.)*

MESOZOIC ERA

Period	Millions of Years Ago	Examples of Life Forms	Length of section
Cretaceous	65	Age of mammals begins. Prosimians, earliest primates develop. Large flightless birds live on the land. Flowering plants are common.	25 cm
	144	There are advanced dinosaurs such as Triceratops, Tyrannosaurus Rex, mammals such as opossums, and flowering plants such as magnolias. Plankton, coral reefs, marine reptiles and ammonoids live in the ocean.	79 cm
Jurassic	208	Reptiles such as crocodiles, turtles, lizards, and dinosaurs dominate the land. Pterosaurs (flying reptiles) and Archaeopteryx as well as varieties of mammals appear. More advanced insects such as flies appear. Marine reptiles such as ichthyosaurs and plesiosaurs live in the ocean.	64 cm
		Extinction at the End of the Triassic Period Up to 75% of marine invertebrate species and some land dwellers vanish. Two recently evolved groups, dinosaurs and mammals, survive. The cause of this extinction is unknown.	
Triassic	248	Reptiles dominate, including ancestors of dinosaurs and mammals. Ferns, gingkoes and conifers appear. Ammonoids dominate the seas.	40 cm

18

Earth's Time Line *(cont.)*

PALEOZOIC ERA

Period	Millions of Years Ago	Examples of Life Forms	Length of section
Permian	290	**Greatest Mass Extinction of All: Nearly all Permian species die.** Reptiles begin to take over. Dinosaur ancestors such as Eryops, Dimetrodon, and Thecondont appear. Insects, giant club mosses, seed ferns and horsetails flourish. Pines and firs appear.	42 cm
Carboniferous	362	Age of amphibians—reptiles, snails, centipedes, cockroaches and giant dragonflies appear. Giant tree-ferns, horsetails, and coral reefs abound.	72 cm
Extinction of Most of World's Fish: Perhaps 70% of invertebrate species perish in late Devonian Period.			
Devonian	418	Small amphibians venture onto land to join flightless insects and spiders. Large spore-bearing plants form the first forests. Age of fishes—jawed and jawless bony fish live in the ocean with trilobites and coral.	46 cm
Supercontinent Gondwanaland drifts over South Pole in Ordovician Period. This brings a long period of glaciation. Early fish arrive, but marine invertebrates and primitive reef builders are hard hit.			
Ordovician	505	No fossils of land animals have been found from this period. Shelled invertebrates develop. Corals, bivalves, and trilobites are among life in the ocean. Jawless armored fish appear.	67 cm
Cambrian	570	Primitive algae and seaweeds, jellyfish, sponges, starfish, worms live in the ocean. Trilobites and brachiopods dominate and coral reefs rise.	65 cm
Precambrian Time	700 900 3,500 4,000 4,600	Worms and jellyfish appear. First oxygen-breathing animals appear in ocean. Life first appears in ocean—single celled algae and bacteria. Primordial sea formed, no life forms. Earth formed from gaseous material spun off the sun.	1.3 m 2 m 26 m 5 m 6 m

Interpreting Earth's Time Line

Name:_____ Date: _____

> You are a paleontologist who is writing a speech to describe the changes which have happened on Earth during the last 4.6 billion years. Answer the questions listed below using the time line and the Earth Time Line chart so you can use this information in your speech.

1. How long did it take for the first life forms to appear on Earth?_____

2. What were the first forms of life and where did they live? _____

   _____

3. What lived in the ocean during the Cambrian and Ordovician Periods? _____

   _____

4. The atmosphere on Earth was very different when it first formed. Gases escaping from below the crust through volcanic vents created this early atmosphere, which had little or no oxygen. What was needed to create the oxygen? (Hint: Earth's oxygen still comes from this source.)

   _____

5. Among the first animals to live on land were the amphibians. They formed a bridge between animals that live only in water and those which live only on land. Explain what an amphibian is and give an example of one.

   _____

   _____

6. Dinosaurs were on Earth at least 150 million years. How does this compare with the length of time humans have been here?_____

   _____

7. What do scientists think caused the end of the dinosaur era about 65 million years ago?_____

   _____

8. At least 99% of all species that have ever lived on Earth have become extinct. Mass extinctions took place several different times. Describe these, beginning with the one at the end of the Triassic Period. Tell when they happened and what effect this had on life on Earth.

   _____

   _____

   _____

   _____

   _____

When Were Dinosaur Fossils First Found?

A Brief History of Dinosaur Discoveries

Dinosaur bones were discovered in China as early as 300 A.D. and described by a Chinese scholar of the time, Chang Qu, who wrote about "dragon bones" which had magical powers. There are also records of American Indians discovering the bones of "giant buffalo" that were thought to give braves good luck during a hunt. Scientists believe the dragon and giant buffalo bones were very likely from dinosaurs.

In 1667, Robert Plot described a gigantic thigh bone found in Oxfordshire, England. Some thought it may have belonged to an elephant brought to England by the Romans, and later it was thought to be from a giant human. Later scientists looked at the picture Robert Plot drew of the bone and decided it was most likely from a thigh bone of *Megalosaurus* (great lizard). At first, scientists thought these were just huge lizards. When they looked closer at the fossil skeletons, they discovered that dinosaurs' legs were under their bodies, not sprawled to the sides like lizards' legs.

Amateur paleontologist and doctor, Gideo Mantell, was one of the first people to suggest that there had been huge reptiles living long ago. His wife discovered unusual teeth and showed them to her husband. He immediately recognized them as fossil teeth from a plant-eater which had been very big. He published a description of the find in 1825 and named the animal *Iguanodon* since it looked as if the teeth had come from an iguana. Dr. Mantell drew the Iguanodon from the few bones he found, showing it walking on four legs and with a horn on its nose. Later it was discovered that the nose horn actually was a thumb claw, and the Iguanodon could walk on two or four feet. When walking on two legs, it leaned forward to counterbalance its body with its tail.

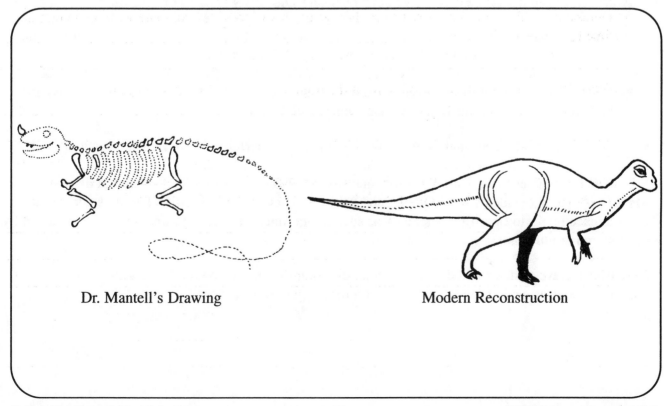

Dr. Mantell's Drawing   Modern Reconstruction

Where Are Dinosaur Fossils Found?

Ms. Frizzle and her students met many different dinosaurs on their trip back in time. The children also made a variety of reports about dinosaurs.

Specimens of dinosaur fossils have been found on every continent, including Antarctica. Plotting their location tells scientists much about the history of dinosaurs and the changes on Earth over millions of years.

Between 1802 and 1860, thousands of fossilized dinosaur tracks were found in Connecticut and were mistaken for prints of giant birds. Dinosaur fossil hunting became popular in the United States after 1877 when news of huge fossil bones found in Colorado and Wyoming spread. Two scientists in particular, Edward Cope and Othneil Marsh, were rivals in trying to find the most fossil bones. They eventually named nearly 130 new species between them, including *Apatosaurus* and *Camarasaurus*. There are many exciting stories about people finding dinosaurs fossils, even recent discoveries like *Seismosaurus* found in 1991. (See Resource section for reference books.)

To the Teacher: Make a transparency of the map on page 23 and ask the students to tell where most of the dinosaur discoveries have been made. (North America, South America, Europe, and China) Explain that there are many more dinosaur discoveries to be made.

Let's see where 18 species of dinosaurs have been found. Most of these appeared in the Ms. Frizzle's students' reports or were seen by them on their field trip back to the time of the dinosaurs.

Materials: large map of North America, showing the states in the U.S., Baja, California, and provinces in Canada; small self-adhesive dots; Dinosaur Discovery Data chart (page 24)

Procedure: Divide among the students the responsibility of plotting the dinosaur information on the map. Use the information from the Dinosaur Discovery Data chart to place dots on the map in locations where dinosaurs have been discovered. Copy the number of the dinosaurs from the chart onto the dot. Plot every discovery, even when more than one location is given for the same dinosaur. Display a copy of the Dinosaur Discovery Data chart and the map.

Closure: Have the students analyze the data on the map to determine where most dinosaur sites are located in the United States and Canada (midwest). Ask them where they think the dig site is that Ms. Frizzle and her students are visiting. (Montana, since it is the only site of the Maiasaura discovery.) Ms. Frizzle and her students see a Dinodontosaurus in the late Triassic Period. Let the students search the reference books to find if there really was such a dinosaur or if this is an imaginary one made up by the author and illustrator.

Extension: Have students add data about other dinosaur discoveries on the North American map and other continents as well. (See Resource section for suggested references.)

Dinosaur Discoveries

The map below shows sites of dinosaur discoveries which have been made on every continent. Some fossil sites are even located in Alaska and Antarctica. New discoveries are continually being made by scientists, as well as by people who just enjoy looking for fossils. A great discovery of a complete Tyrannosaur skeleton was found in eastern Montana in 1988 by Kathy Wankel, a rancher in the area.

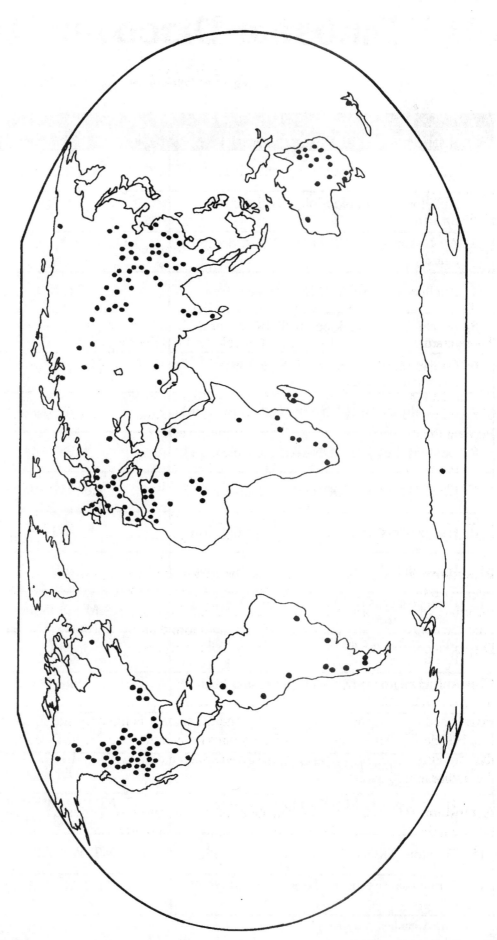

Dinosaur Discovery Data

(Most of this data is from *The Ultimate Dinosaur Book* by David Lambert)

Name (pronunciation and meaning)	Found	Lived MYA*
1. Allosaurus (al-oh-SORE-us: other lizard)	CO, MT, NM, OK, SD, UT, WY	156–130
2. Ankylosaurus (an-kie-loh-SORE-us: stiff lizard)	CA	68
3. Apatosaurus (ah-PAT-oh-SORE-us: deceptive lizard)	CO; UT; OK; WY; Baja, CA Mex.	156–150
4. Anchisaurus (AN-ki-SORE-us: near lizard)	CT, MA	194
5. Brachiosaurus (brak-ee-oh-SORE-us: arm lizard)	CO, WY, UT	153–113
6. Camarasaurus (kam-are-ah-SORE-us: chambered lizard)	CO, UT, WY	155–150
7. Coelophysis (SEE-loh-FIF-sis: hollow form)	AZ, NM	225
8. Deinonychus (die-NON-i-kus: terrible claw)	MT, WY	113
9. Diplodocus (di-PLOH-de-kus: double-beam)	CO, UT, WY	150
10. Hadrosaurus (HAD-roh-SORE-us: big lizard)	NJ	67–65
11. Iguanodon (ig-WHA-noh-don: iguana tooth)	SD	140–110
12. Lambeosaurus (LAM-bee-oh-SORE-us: Lambe's lizard)	MT, Alberta	75
13. Maiasaura (MY-ah-SORE-ah: good mother lizard)	MT	80–75
14. Seismosaurus (SIZE-moh-SORE-us: earth-shaking lizard)	NM	150
15. Stegosaurus (STEG-oh-SORE-us: roof lizard)	CO, UT, WY	150
16. Struthiomimus (STRUTH-ee-oh-MEEM-us: ostrich lizard)	Alberta	73
17. Triceratops (try-SERRA-tops: three-horned face)	MT, ND, SD, WY, Alberta, Saskatchewan	67–65
18. Troodon (TROH-oh-don; wounding tooth)	MT, WY, Alberta	80–65
19. Tyrannosaurus (tie-RAN-oh-Sore-us; tyrant lizard)	CO, MT, NM, WY, Alberta, Saskatchewan	68–65

MYA=million years ago

How Are Dinosaurs Grouped?

Ms. Frizzle has mentioned names of some of the groups of dinosaurs to her students. When they started in the Late Triassic Period, she told them they would see early dinosaurs. Scientists call these *Prosauropods,* meaning "before sauropods." Later, when they travel into the Late Jurassic Period, she points out the *sauropods,* which were huge plant-eaters with long necks and tails. The largest animals that ever lived on land were sauropods.

The Friz and her students also saw pre-historic animals which lived in the Cretaceous Period but were not dinosaurs. These were flying reptiles such as the *Pteranodons* and animals which swam in the oceans, like the giant turtle *Archelon, Elasmosaurus,* and the giant fish *Ichthyosaur.*

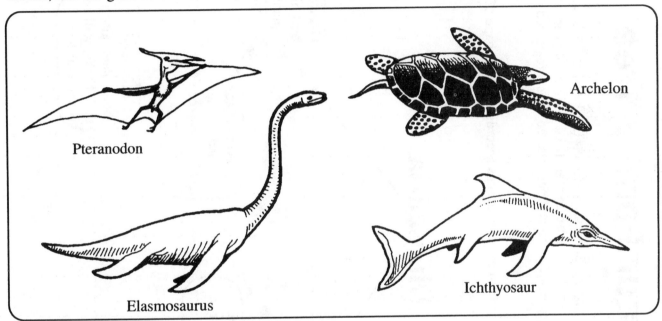

Pteranodon

Archelon

Elasmosaurus

Ichthyosaur

Let's see how scientists classify the dinosaurs into groups.

To the Teacher: The students should work in small groups to sort the dinosaur pictures shown on pages 27–31. *Each group will need a set of the pictures which have been cut out for them and have the identification removed.*

Materials: set of the dinosaurs (without identification) shown on pages 27–31, transparencies of Dinosaur Family Tree (page 26) and Dinosaur Identification pages 27–31.

Procedure: Divide students into groups and distribute a set of dinosaur pictures to each group. Have them sort the dinosaurs into family groups according to any method they devise based on the physical characteristics (answers will vary). When finished, have one person from each group describe how they sorted the dinosaurs.

Closure: Explain the family tree of dinosaurs to illustrate how scientists divide the dinosaurs. Show the transparencies of the dinosaurs which have been identified according to their scientific grouping. Point out the physical features used to classify these dinosaurs. Have the students compare these transparencies with their systems of classification and find which were the most accurate.

Dinosaur Family Tree

A British scientist, Sir Richard Owen, was the first to use the term *dinosauria* in 1841. The word "dinosaur" means terrible lizard. They were not lizards, but most scientists now agree they were reptiles. These animals lived millions of years ago and were all land animals. None lived in water or flew, except possibly Archeopteryx, which is sometimes referred to as a feathered dinosaur because its hands, hips, legs, and skull were very like the Theropods.

As more dinosaurs were found, scientists began to classify them into two groups according to the shape of their hip bones. These were further divided as shown in the diagram below:

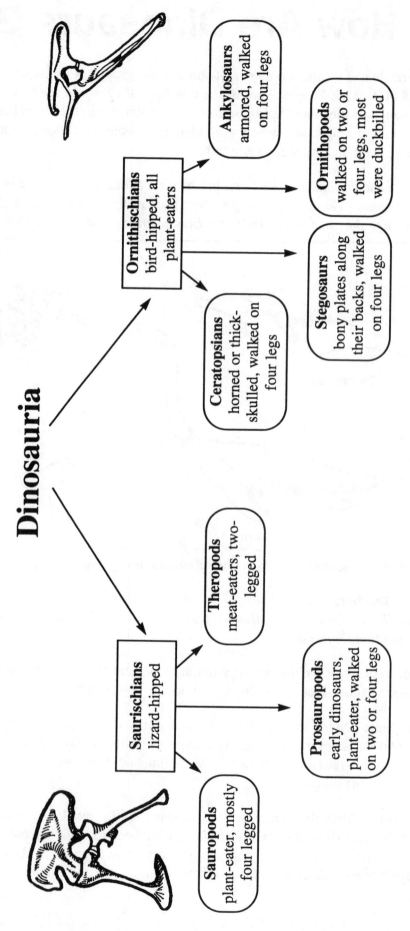

Dinosauria

Ornithischians bird-hipped, all plant-eaters

Ankylosaurs armored, walked on four legs

Ornithopods walked on two or four legs, most were duckbilled

Stegosaurs bony plates along their backs, walked on four legs

Ceratopsians horned or thick-skulled, walked on four legs

Saurischians lizard-hipped

Theropods meat-eaters, two-legged

Prosauropods early dinosaurs, plant-eater, walked on two or four legs

Sauropods plant-eater, mostly four legged

26

Saurischians

Prosauropod

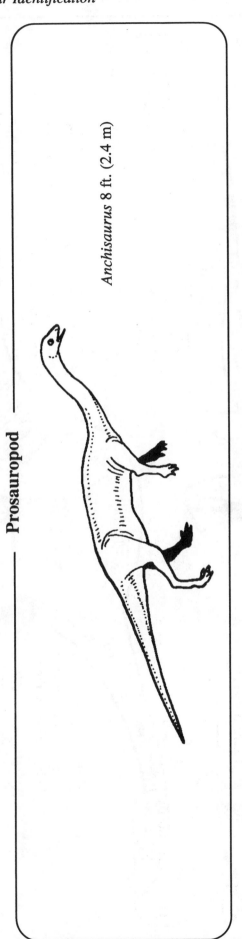

Anchisaurus 8 ft. (2.4 m)

Sauripods

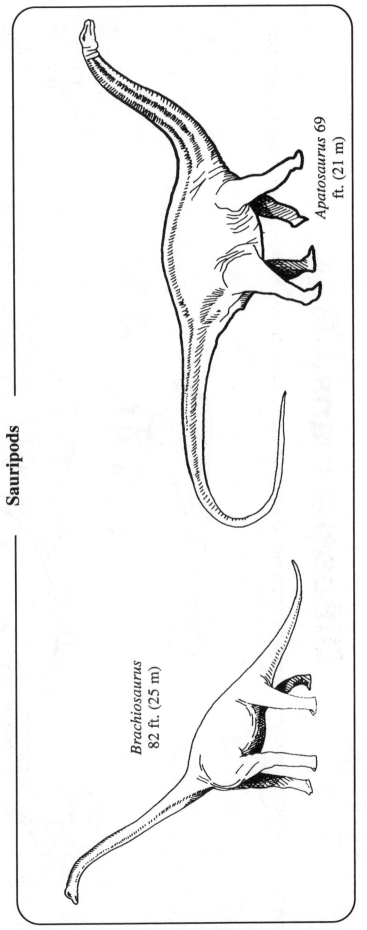

Apatosaurus 69 ft. (21 m)

Brachiosaurus 82 ft. (25 m)

Saurischians *(cont.)*

Sauripods *(cont.)*

Camarasaurus
59 ft. (18 m)

Diplodocus
89 ft. (27 m)

Seismosaurus
150 ft. (40 m)

Saurischians (cont.)

Theropods

Struthiomimus
13 ft. (4 m)

Allosaurus
36 ft. (11 m)

Deinonychus
10 ft. (3 m)

Troodon
7 ft. (2 m)

Coelophysis
10 ft. (3 m)

Tyrannosaurs
39 ft. (12 m)

Ornithiscians

Ceratopsians

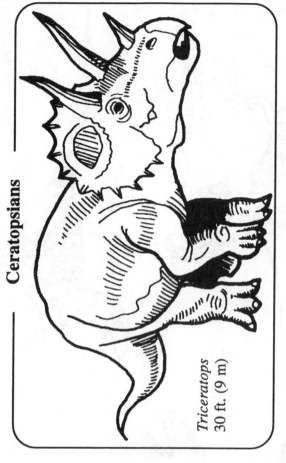

Triceratops
30 ft. (9 m)

Ankylosaurs

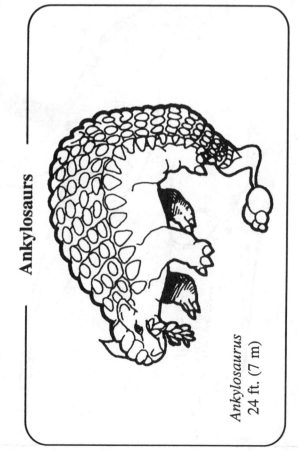

Ankylosaurus
24 ft. (7 m)

Stegosaurs

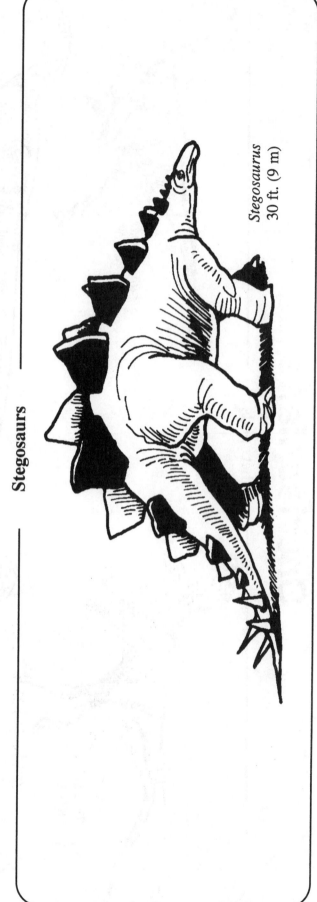

Stegosaurus
30 ft. (9 m)

Ornithiscians *(cont.)*

Ornithopods

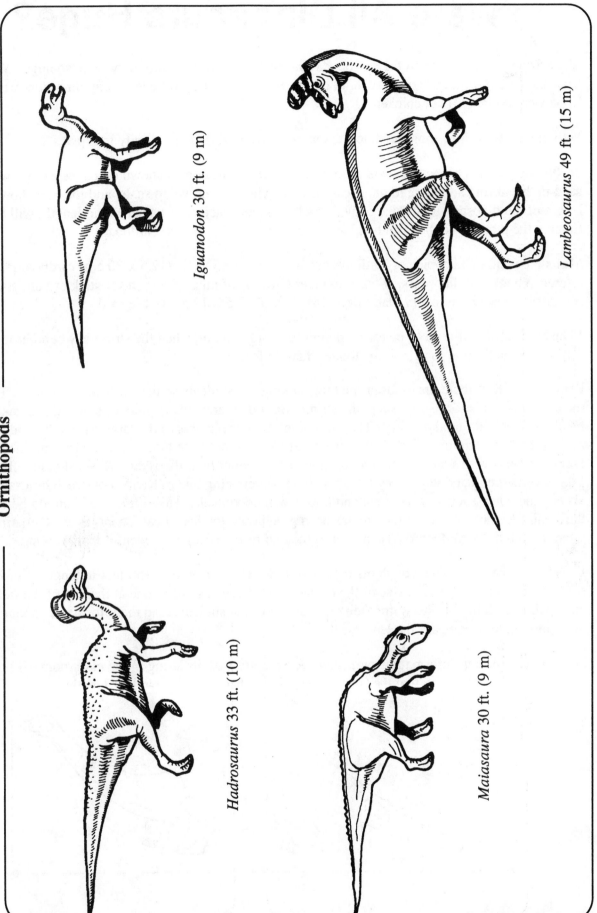

Iguanodon 30 ft. (9 m)

Lambeosaurus 49 ft. (15 m)

Hadrosaurus 33 ft. (10 m)

Maiasaura 30 ft. (9 m)

Were All Dinosaurs Huge?

Ms. Frizzle's students found the sauropods impossible to miss because they were so huge. When you hear the word *dinosaurs,* you may think of enormous animals. Although many dinosaurs were huge, some were no larger than chickens.

Let's find out just how long the dinosaurs were that you sorted into family groups.

To the Teacher: This activity will require a copy of the dinosaurs shown on pages 27–31, which were used in the sorting activity earlier. Please note they are not drawn to scale, and the size shown is the length of the dinosaur. Only one copy of each dinosaur, including its name and length, will be needed. Enlarge the pictures so they can be glued on 5" x 8" (12.5 x 20 cm) cardboard.

Materials: enlarged copies of 19 dinosaurs, 19 pieces of 5" x 8" (12.5 x 20 cm) cardboard*, glue, reference books on dinosaurs, at least 800 feet (240 m) of thick string, meter stick or yard stick, scissors, Dinosaur Discovery Data (page 24), 3" x 5" (7.5 x 12.5 cm) file card

*The cardboard will need to be thick enough to avoid bending when the string is wound around it. This is especially true for dinosaurs longer than 20 feet.

Procedure: Distribute the dinosaur pictures among the students so they will work in pairs. Provide the other materials for them, except the string. Set up an area where pairs of students can take turns measuring and cutting the string. They should glue their pictures to the large cardboard and then prepare brief descriptions of their dinosaurs. Students should use the reference material, including the Dinosaur Discoveries chart to find more information about their dinosaurs. They should tell where the fossils were found and when they lived on Earth. Interesting bits of trivia about each dinosaur should also be included, such as what it ate and how it defended itself. This information should be written on the small file card. After the picture has been glued onto the heavy cardboard, attach the string and wind it around the cardboard. Tie a knot in the end of the string to prevent it from fraying.

Closure: Take the students outdoors to a large field which is at least 150 feet in length. Have the students line up according to size of their dinosaurs. Draw a starting line at the end of the field and let each pair stretch out the string for their dinosaur. Let the students read the information about their dinosaur and then compare the lengths.

Display the dinosaur information cards and each picture with its string in the classroom. If possible, mount them in such a way that the strings can be stretched out to show their lengths.

Were All Dinosaurs Huge? *(cont.)*

Ms. Frizzle's class saw an Allosaurus attack a Stegosaurus. Since the Stegosaurus was wounded, it could not fight off the Allosaurus and ended up becoming its dinner.

Let's see how big the Allosaurus is compared to the Stegosaurus and to you.

Materials: transparency pictures of the Allosaurus and Stegosaurus, two overhead projectors, a large room at least 36 feet long, long measuring tape

Procedure: You will need a large wall for this projection; it should be at least 36 feet long. Make a copy of the picture of Allosaurus and Stegosaurus shown below. Separate the dinosaurs and enlarge them as big as possible on a 8 ½" x 11" (21 x 28 cm) paper and then make a transparency of each of these pictures. Place the Allosaurus picture on one projector and back it away from the wall until the picture is 36 feet long. Put the Stegosaurus on the other projector and make it 30 feet long. The Allosaurus should be in pursuit of the Stegosaurus with some space between them. Point out that these dinosaurs were about the same size and were both huge animals.

Closure: Let the students imagine they are on the *Magic School Bus*® Time Machine and have gone back in time to the Jurassic Period with Ms. Frizzle's students. Suddenly, they find themselves between these two dinosaurs. Have students volunteer to stand in the picture between the dinosaurs so they can see for themselves how small they are compared to the dinosaurs.

Extension: Have students write an illustrated story to tell what they think it would be like to have these dinosaurs still on Earth today. Bind their stories into a book and share it with other students, perhaps putting it on display in the school library.

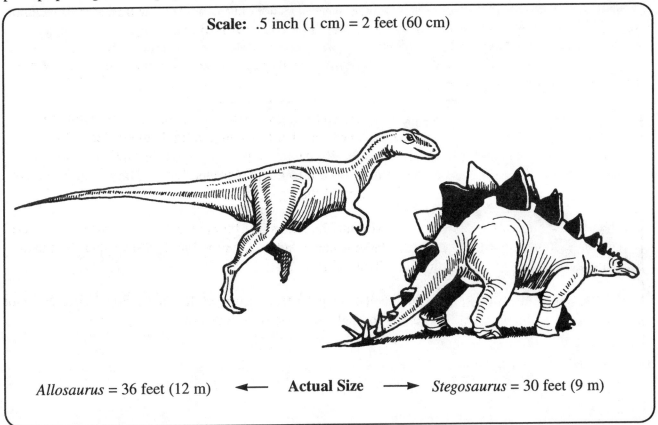

Scale: .5 inch (1 cm) = 2 feet (60 cm)

Allosaurus = 36 feet (12 m)   ←   **Actual Size**   →   *Stegosaurus* = 30 feet (9 m)

Were All Dinosaurs Huge? *(cont.)*

The paleontologists Ms. Frizzle and her students visited were excavating the fossil remains of a Maiasaura dinosaur and were searching for the nests of these animals. The Frizz went back in time to see if she and her students could find the Maiasauras and locate their nests. Not only did they find the nesting site, but they also found eggs and babies in the nests, as well as parents taking care of them. Suddenly, the Troodons entered the nesting area, and a great battle began between these meat-eaters and the Maiasauras trying to protect their babies. A sudden sandstorm blew in, killing all these animals and covering them with layers of sand. This sand would later become hardened into stone, and the bones and eggs of the dinosaurs would become fossils.

Dr. John (Jack) Horner, a real paleontologist who has been hunting fossils since he was a child, has discovered the largest nesting site of these animals in Montana. He discovered eggs, embryos inside the eggs, and baby Maiasauras. He even found fossils of the Troodon dinosaur, which most likely was eating the babies. He wrote a story about the Maiasaura for young readers.

Let's read Dr. Horner's book *Maia: A Dinosaur Grows Up* (see Resources) and learn how these gentle animals lived during the Cretaceous Period, about 80 million years ago. You will also learn of other dinosaurs which lived in the same location and time period.

Materials: *Maia: A Dinosaur Grows Up,* transparencies of the Troodon (page 29) and Maiasaura (page 31), two overhead projectors, room at least 40 feet (12 m) long, long tape measure

Procedure: Read the book aloud to the students and show them the illustrations. Stop reading periodically to check for understanding and allow students to ask questions and discuss the story.

Closure: Enlarge the pictures of the Troodon and Maiasaura below. Make a transparency of each of them. Take the students to a room where the images of Troodon and Maiasaura can be projected near each other to compare their size. Students will notice that the Maiasaura is much larger than the Troodon. Discuss why the Troodon was only eating the babies. Let the students compare their size to these two dinosaurs.

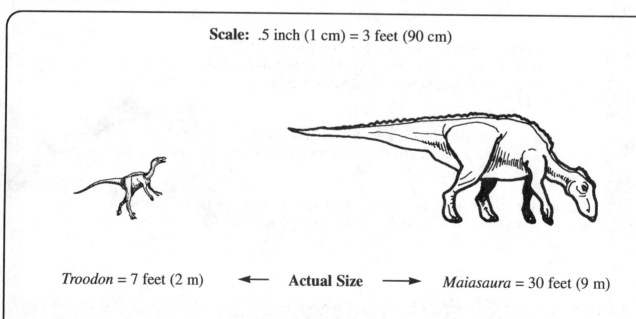

Scale: .5 inch (1 cm) = 3 feet (90 cm)

Troodon = 7 feet (2 m) ← **Actual Size** → *Maiasaura* = 30 feet (9 m)

Which Dinosaurs Lived at the Same Time?

Ms. Frizzle and her students discovered that different dinosaurs lived at different periods of time. For example, they found the Maiasaura lived in the Cretaceous Period, long after the Allosaurus and Stegosaurus had disappeared.

Let's put the 19 dinosaurs on the time line you made earlier to see which ones lived in the same time periods.

To the Teacher: Divide part of the Mesozoic Era of the time line into 5 million year sections. Measure 40 cm from the beginning of the time line and mark this spot, which is the end of the Cretaceous Period 65 million years ago. Mark off the next 185 cm in 5 cm sections. Each section represents 5 million years. Identify each mark beginning with 65, then 70, 75, . . .225 to indicate millions of years. These sections will be used when students place their dinosaurs on the time line according to the period in which they lived.

Materials: Dinosaur Discovery Data chart (page 24), time line, copies of the 19 dinosaurs on pages 27–31, 1 cm grid graph paper for each dinosaur, felt pens or crayons

Procedure: Divide the dinosaurs among the students and provide them with pictures of their dinosaurs and 1 cm grid paper. Use a scale of 2 cm = 1 m and have students calculate how long their paper must be to show that length. Let the students sketch the outline of the dinosaur on the 1 cm grid paper. The overhead projector maybe used with transparencies of dinosaurs larger than 59 feet (18 m) long to enlarge them by projecting them on graph paper.

Only fossil prints of dinosaur skin have been found; thus, no one knows what color they were. Students may want to use the colors shown in *The Magic School Bus*® book or those found in reference books. Be sure each drawing has the name of the dinosaur on it.

Closure: After the dinosaur pictures have been completed, let students use the Dinosaur Discovery Data chart to help them place the dinosaurs near the time line and connect them to it with string.

Extension: Let students make three-dimensional scenes of Dinosaur Days, depicting several dinosaurs which lived during the same period, as well as the plants that lived at that time. This can be done with paper cut-outs or clay.

Earth's Time Line Flipbook

When Ms. Frizzle and her class traveled back in time, they not only found that animals and plants were different from those of today, but the climate was different also. Look for Ms. Frizzle's pet iguana showing maps of what the Earth looked like at various times of the geologic history.

Geologic Background: The Earth is about 4.6 billion years old. Spun off the sun at first, it was a gaseous ball which slowly cooled to a liquid. About 4.3 billion years ago, a solid crust formed on the outside. Below this crust, the Earth gets hotter and hotter as you go toward the center.

In 1912, a German meteorologist and geophysicist, Alfred Wegener, suggested that the continents had drifted and were split off from a giant prehistoric continent he named *Pangaea*. People laughed at him since it seemed impossible for continents to move. Later, scientists with modern equipment began to gather evidence that proved his theory. A drilling rig aboard a ship brought up from the ocean floor rock core samples that were not all the same age. A long ridge was discovered running north and south along the Atlantic Ocean floor and into the Indian Ocean. Rock samples from either side of the ridge grew older as the scientists moved away from the ridge toward the continents. Fossils of dinosaurs found along the western coast of Africa matched those found on the eastern coast of South America. They clearly had been able to walk between these continents at one time. If you look at a map of these two continents, they appear to be puzzle pieces which could fit together. Scientists now have enough evidence to conclude that all the continents were once joined in one supercontinent.

Let's see how the Earth has changed over the past 570 million years.

To the Teacher: The latitudes of 30° north and south, as well as the equator, are drawn on the pictures of the Earth in this flipbook. The latitude lines do not remain in the same position on each drawing since different views of the planet are shown to enable all the continents to be visible. These lines provide reference points for the changing location of the continents.

Materials: Earth's flipbook pictures and information on pages 39–42, scissors, glue, wide clear packing tape, 12 unlined file cards 3" x 5" (7.5 cm x 12.5 cm), transparencies of pages 39-42

Procedure: Distribute copies of pages 39–42 to each student. Use the transparencies of these pages while students follow along on their copies to compare the information with the drawings. Have the students cut out the flipbook pictures and information. Glue one picture to each file card in the lower right corner. Glue the matching information for that picture to the back of the card. Place the 12 cards in a stack by laying the most recent time card on a table and putting the next earlier date on top of it, leaving about ¼ inch (½ cm) edge sticking out. Continue doing this until all cards are stacked like stairs, ending with the oldest period as the top card. Test the flipbook by holding the cards firmly in place with one hand and using the other hand to flip rapidly from the first picture to the last. The continents should appear to move relative to the equator and each other. Use the clear tape to keep the cards together by placing one long piece over the edge where you held them together, then another around the cards near the same end.

Earth's Time Line Flipbook *(cont.)*

Closure: Read the information for each geologic period; then flip the cards slowly to see how the continents moved during these 570 million years. Use the information in the Geologic Background on page 36 to explain how scientists know the history of Earth's continental drift.

Show the map on page 38 depicting what scientists think the Earth will look like 50 million years from now. Compare the location and shapes of the continents to what they are today. Be sure students see that Baja California in Mexico and part of California are now their own separate continent and have moved north, near what is now Oregon and Washington. North America has drifted into the Asian continent near Siberia and has separated from South America. Discuss how this move will affect the climate in North America. Note how a section of Africa has pulled away to form a separate continent. Discuss the other changes which are visible in the continents.

Extension: Make enlarged copies of the flipbook pictures and information to display near the corresponding periods on Earth's Time Line.

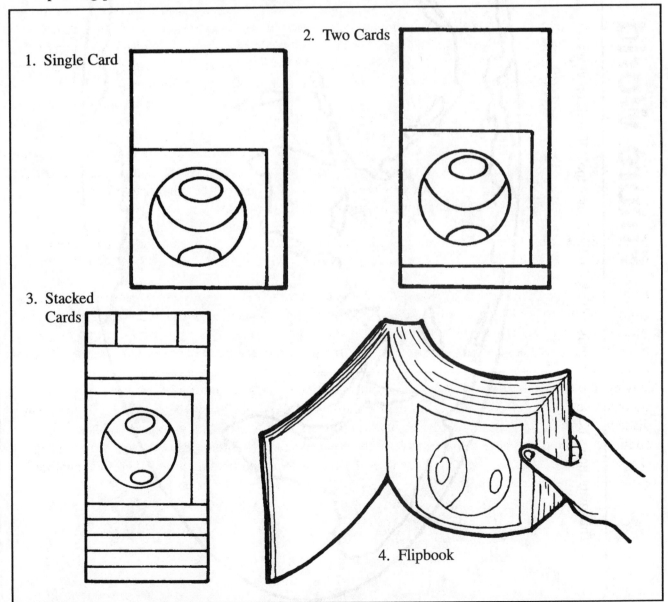

1. Single Card

2. Two Cards

3. Stacked Cards

4. Flipbook

Future World

This map shows how the scientists think the Earth may look 50 million years from now as the continents continue to move.

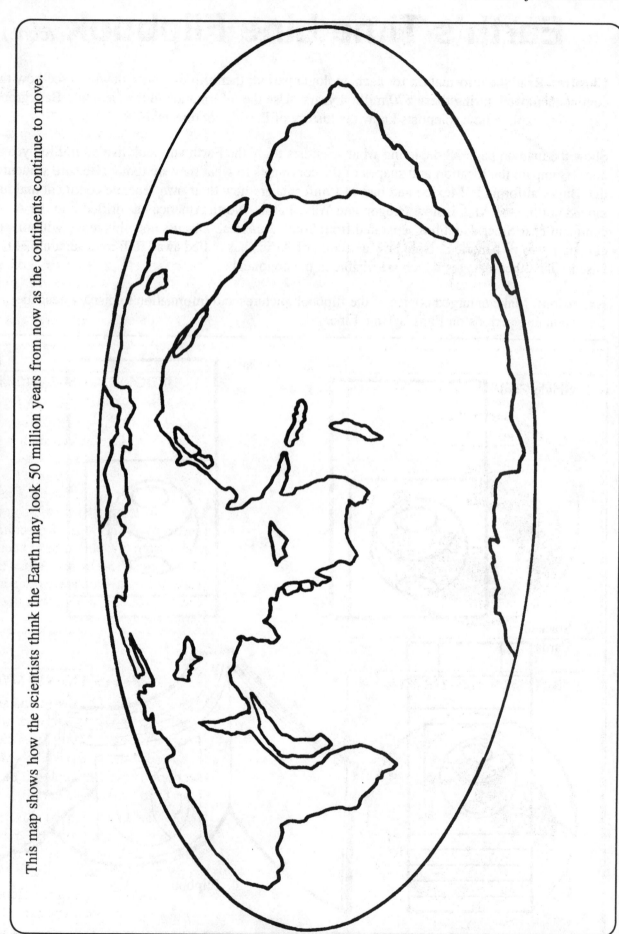

Earth's Time Line Flipbook

CAMBRIAN 570–505 MYA

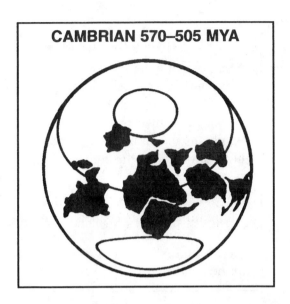

CAMBRIAN 570–505 MYA

The outlines of continents are shown as we know them today, but most of them would actually be submerged beneath a shallow sea at this time. Life only exists in the oceans during this period.

The climate is generally warmer than it is today since most continents were near the equator, even Antarctica. A supercontinent—*Gondwanaland*—was formed by South America, Africa, India, Antarctica, and Australia.

ORDOVICIAN 505–440 MYA

ORDOVICIAN 505–440 MYA

The supercontinent *Laurentia* is formed by North America and Greenland. Gondwanaland has moved deep into Antarctica latitudes. Northwest Africa is over the South Pole and is very near South America. The climate here is so cold that ice sheets cover this area. Ice-scratched rocks from this period have been discovered in northwest Africa and eastern South America, evidence that these continents were once covered by ice.

SILURIAN 440–418 MYA

SILURIAN 440–418 MYA

North America and Greenland are beginning to collide into what will become Europe. North America ends at eastern Nevada and Idaho. More sections of the continent will be added later from Gondwanaland.

In the southern continent, Africa, Gondwanaland, and South America were drifting north while Antarctica and Australia headed south.

Melting southern ice sheets flooded continents with shallow seas.

Earth's Time Line Flipbook *(cont.)*

DEVONIAN 418–362 MYA

DEVONIAN 418–362 MYA

Eastern North America, Greenland, and western Europe are one continent. Fossils in the rocks laid down at this time show freshwater fish and the first amphibians which live in Greenland, which is located at the equator during this period.

Gondwanaland is moving north, pushing minicontinents ahead of it. Only a narrow sea separates South America and Africa from North America and Europe.

CARBONIFEROUS 362–290 MYA

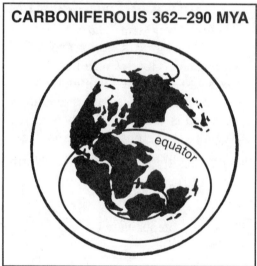

CARBONIFEROUS 362–290 MYA

North America and Europe collide with the northern edges of Gondwanaland—the part containing South America and Africa. By 350 million years ago, they join the northern and southern continents to form *Pangaea*.

Southern continents lie across the South Pole. By the end of this period ice covers Antarctica, parts of Australia, and much of southern South America, Africa, and India.

PERMIAN 290–248 MYA

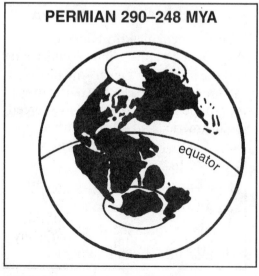

PERMIAN 290–248MYA

All continents lay jammed together as the supercontinent *Pangaea*, which is surrounded by a single ocean. As Pangaea moves north, glaciers retreat south in South America, Africa, and India. Ice covers Antarctica as it crosses the South Pole and also areas of Australia.

As land sections are formed together, they create mountain ranges which still exist today in southern Europe and southeastern North America.

Earth's Time Line Flipbook *(cont.)*

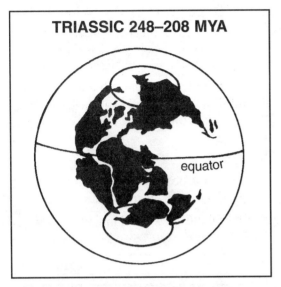

TRIASSIC 248–208 MYA

The Pangaea landmass has drifted north. North America, Europe, and northwest Africa are locked together. Much of North America and Europe are having tropical weather.

Gondwanaland is no longer at the South Pole; southern ice sheets have all melted. The world climate ranges from warm to mild, and deserts are extensive.

Ancestors of the dinosaurs and Mammals first appeared.

JURASSIC 208–144 MYA

World climates are mostly warm, and land is mostly low since earlier mountain ranges have been worn down. Dinosaurs wander overland across the world they share with early birds and mammals.

Pangaea has started to break up. North America is pushing away from northwest Africa. Africa and South America are pushing away from each other. Antarctica and Australia are separating.

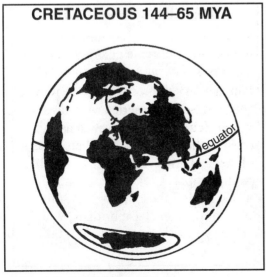

CRETACEOUS 144–65 MYA

Pangea is breaking into Laurasia (north) and Gondwanaland (south) and both these supercontinents are also cracking up. The spreading rifts in the floor of the Atlantic Ocean have forced South America and Africa further apart. They have also separated Greenland from northern Europe.

The climate is mostly warm and mild. Flowering plants are spreading. Something happens at the end of this period, killing the dinosaurs and many other creatures, but not all perish.

Earth's Time Line Flipbook *(cont.)*

TERTIARY 65–25 MYA

TERTIARY 65–25 MYA

The continents are located near their locations today. Western North America is moving east overriding the crust on the ocean floor, pushing up the Rocky Mountains. North American is now separated from Europe.

Africa has forced its way north. India continues to drift north toward Asia.

Australia and New Zealand are moving north.

TERTIARY 25–2 MYA

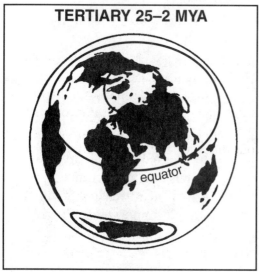

TERTIARY 25–2 MYA

Continents have almost reached their present places, and crashing plates are pushing up great modern mountain ranges.

North and South America are adjoined by material which has been pushed up from the ocean floor. The Baja peninsula and the piece of California which is now west of the San Andreas Fault has torn away from Mexico and moved north to join to the rest of California during this period.

QUATERNARY 2–0 MYA

QUATERNARY 2–0 MYA

Ice sheets cover much of the northern areas. As the climate changes, ice appeares and disappears in many ice ages. This changes the shape of the land.

Land bridges form between Alaska and Siberia, mainland Asia and Indonesia, New Guinea and Australia, and the British Isles and mainland Europe during these ice ages. Animals could move over these bridges, which flooded when the ice melted 10,000 years ago.

Undiscovered Dinosaurs

After Ms. Frizzle and her students returned from their exciting field trip back in time, they presented a variety of exhibits for Visitors Day. They even made up their own dinosaurs, like the *Bananasaurus Rex* and *Sockosaur.*

New species of dinosaurs are still being discovered. This means there are unknown dinosaurs still uncovered. Think of all you have learned as you studied the dinosaurs and design a new dinosaur which may be discovered in the future. Perhaps you will be the one to find it first!

Write a description of your dinosaur and include important information about it, such as the following:

- ✧ Where did it live and what was the climate like?
- ✧ Was it a meat-eater or plant-eater? What kind of teeth did it have?
- ✧ How big was it?
- ✧ Did it belong to the Saurischians (lizard-hipped) or Ornithischians (bird-hipped) group?
- ✧ Is it the relative of an earlier dinosaur? If so, how does it resemble that dinosaur?
- ✧ In which period did it live, and what other dinosaurs were its neighbors?
- ✧ What name can you give it that will describe it?

Write your description as a newspaper article which will give as much detail as possible to the public about this new dinosaur discovery. Use the information on the Dinosaur Family Tree (page 26), as well as the Dinosaur Discovery Data chart (page 24) to help you. On another paper, make several drawings of your dinosaur to show what it looked like, how it moved, and the type of teeth it had. Show what the land looked like where it lived and include a few of its neighbor dinosaurs. Be sure to label the parts of your drawing so your readers will know the names of your dinosaur and others shown in the picture.

What Did You Learn?

You have learned a lot about dinosaurs since beginning this unit; now is your chance to show just how much you have learned. Return to pages four and five where you tried to show which of the animals in the pictures were dinosaurs. Do this activity again, using what you know now to pick out the dinosaurs from the non-dinosaurs. Compare your answers with those you gave at the beginning of the unit. Did you learn a lot about dinosaurs?

Now, it is your turn to climb aboard *The Magic School Bus*® Time Machine and zoom back to the days when dinosaurs roamed the land. You want to begin your journey in an area where you know you will be able to find them.

Which state should you visit to begin this journey through time and why?_____

_____

Write a story about this adventure, describing the dinosaurs you visit and how they live. Use another piece of paper to make drawings showing the reader what you have described. Color the picture when you are finished.

My Trip Back to the Days of the Dinosaurs

Related Books and Periodicals

Abrams, Michael. "Giant Argentineans." *Discover,* January 1996. This article describes the discovery of the largest dinosaur ever found in Argentina, weighing perhaps 100 tons.

Benton, Michael. *The Dinosaur Encyclopedia: A Handbook for Dinosaur Enthusiasts of All Ages.* Simon and Schuster Books for Young Readers, NY, 1984. Topics ranging from describing dinosaurs to methods used to date them and information about dig sites are covered in this book.

Cole, Joanna. *The Magic School Bus® in the Time of the Dinosaurs.* Scholastic, Inc., 1994. This is another adventure of the zany teacher, Ms. Frizzle. The students in her class travel back in time to when dinosaurs roamed the earth. What better way to study them?

Currie, Philip, J. "The Great Dinosaur Egg Hunt." *National Geographic,* May 1996. An exciting find of dinosaur eggs in China reveals embryos and information on size comparison of the young and adult of the same species.

Digging into Dinosaurs. Ranger Rick's NatureScope. Natural Wildlife Federation, 1400 16th Street, NY, Washington, DC 10036-2266 (800)588-1650, 1989. This is an activity book designed for K–8, which includes stories about dinosaurs.

Dinosaurs: A Fold-Out Book. Rand McNally, 1995. This is an excellent 7-foot, double-sided fold-out depicting early ocean animals, reptiles, and dinosaurs.

Dixon, Dougal, et al. *The Macmillan Illustrated Encyclopedia of Dinosaurs and Prehistoric Animals.* Macmillan, 1988. This is a well written resource regarding fish, amphibians, reptiles, birds, and early mammals of prehistoric time.

Dixon, Dougal. *The New Dinosaurs: An Alternative Evolution.* Salem House Pub., 1988. The author imagines what might have happened if dinosaurs had not become extinct. (It can be used to inspire students as they try to create their own present day dinosaurs).

Eyewitness Visual Dictionaries of Dinosaurs. Dorling Kindersley, London, 1993. This contains colorful drawings of dinosaurs and the continents during the Triassic, Jurassic, and Cretaceous periods. The anatomy and size of each dinosaur is given—an easy-to-use reference.

Gardom, Tim and Angela Milner. *The Book of Dinosaurs: The Natural History Museum Guide.* Prima Publishing, Rocklin, CA, 1993. This is a well illustrated book that brings these creatures to life, containing interesting stories of early discoveries—an excellent reference for both teacher and upper grade students.

Gillette, J. Lynett. *The Search for Seismosaurus.* Dial Books for Young Readers, 375 Hudson St., NY, NY. 10014, 1994. The book describes the exciting discovery of remains of a 150 foot (45 m) long Seismosaurus "Giant Shaker" in New Mexico.

Gore, Rick. "Extinctions." *National Geographic,* vol. 175, No. 6, June 1989. (800)447-0647. At least five worldwide catastrophes have erased millions of animal species since life began on Earth. This article includes a graph illustrating which species decreased or were eliminated while others flourished. This issue also includes a poster of dinosaurs.

Related Books and Periodicals *(cont.)*

Horner, John, and John R Gorman. *Maia: A Dinosaur Grows Up.* Running Press, Phila., PA, 1989. In this charming story, Dr. Horner uses his discovery of one of the largest fossilized sites of Maiasaur dinosaur eggs to describe how they lived.

Horner, John, and Don Lessem. *The Complete T. Rex.* Simon and Schuster, 1993. An outstanding resource for teachers, as well as older students, this book gives the latest information about perhaps the favorite dinosaur of all.

Jaroff, Leon. "A Double Whammy?" *Time,* January 9, 1995. This article discusses recent findings by NASA which help to support the theory that an impact from a comet or asteroid could have discharged enough dust and debris into the upper atmosphere to bring about drastic climatic change about 65 million years ago.

Lambert, David. *The Ultimate Dinosaur Book.* Dorling Kindersley, 1993. A beautifully illustrated book covering physical details of 168 dinosaurs. This is an outstanding reference source.

Lessem, Don. "Secrets of the Gobi Desert." *Discover,* June 1989. Roy Chapman Andrews was the first to discover dinosaur eggs, from Protoceratops, in the Gobi Desert of China in the 1920s. Scientists are again returning to this area, making further exciting discoveries of the animals which roamed there millions of years ago.

Munsart, Craig A. *Investigating Science with Dinosaurs.* Teacher Ideas Press, P.O. Box 6633, Englewood, CO 80155-6633, (800)237-6124, 1993. This large book (249 pages) is filled with activities to help students learn more about dinosaurs. It also contains a glossary, pronunciation guide, and extensive bibliography.

Owen, Ellis. *Prehistoric Animals: The Extraordinary Story of Life Before Man.* Octopus Books LTD., 1975. This book is beautifully illustrated with realistic pictures, including animals such as trilobites, fish, amphibians, dinosaurs, and mammals.

Parker, Steve. *The Practical Paleontologist.* Simon and Schuster, Inc., 1990. A great resource book for teachers and older students. The topics cover the history of paleontology, as well as where fossils are found and how they are extracted and then reconstructed. It also provides details of the evolution of life through geologic time from the beginning of the planet.

Sattler, H.R. *The New Illustrated Dinosaur Dictionary.* Beech Tree Paperback Books, NY, 1993. Dinosaurs from A to Z are included in this dictionary which also defines their names, tells when and where they lived, and provides physical information regarding length and weight.

Schatz, Dennis. *Dinosaurs: A Journey Through Time.* Pacific Science Center, 220 Second Ave. North, Seattle, WA 98109, 1987. This book has great hands-on activities which include matching games, construction of dinosaurs, and a room-sized time line.

Sereno, Paul. "Africa's Dinosaur Castaways." *National Geographic,* Vol. 189, No. 6, June 1996. This article tells of the recent discovery of Carcharodontosaurus, which lived about 90 million years ago in the Sahara desert. It was a slightly larger close relative of T. Rex.

Related Books and Periodicals *(cont.)*

Shipman, Pat. "Dinosaur Nests: Bringing Up Baby." *Discover,* August 1988. Paleontologist Jack Horner discovers the extensive nesting sites of dinosaurs in Montana, finding fossil remains of egg shells, embryos, baby dinosaurs, and eggs of predators.

VanCleave, Janice. *Dinosaurs for Every Kid.* John Wiley & Sons, Inc., 1994. Ideas for activities and projects containing a list of materials, instructions, expected results, and explanations.

Webster, Donovan. "Dinosaurs of the Gobi." *National Geographic*, July 1996. This is the exciting recent discovery of Oviraptor eggs and fossils which show evidence that these dinosaurs cared for their young in nests.

Wexo, John B. *Zoobooks: Dinosaurs.* Zoobooks, 9820 Willow Creek Rd., Suite 300, San Diego, CA 92131-1112, 1985. Illustrations depict the process of excavating dinosaurs, reconstructing the specimens, and comparing different species. Theories of how dinosaurs died and their relation to today's birds are included in this easy-to-read reference.

Related Materials

Carolina Biological Supply Co., 2700 York Rd., Burlington, NC 27215 (800)334-5551. Supplies simulated fossil dig kits using real or replicas of fossils, also a variety of videos on fossil dig sites and prehistoric animals.

Delta Education, P.O. Box 3000, Nashua, NH 03061-3000 (800)442-5444. Science modules on prehistoric life and Earth movements; kits include a teacher's guide. Request a science catalog.

DK Multimedia, Distributed by Houghton Mifflin, 1-800-225-3362. The Eyewitness Virtual Reality Series, (CD-ROM) *Dinosaur Hunter*. See the world from the perspective of a dinosaur or an archeologist. (Windows or Macintosh)

Dinosaur-Digging Programs: The Museum of the Rockies in Bozeman, Montana, runs week-long dinosaur digs for children aged 11 and older and shorter programs for families. (406)994-2251. Dinamation International operates family programs for children and their parents. (800)547-0503.

Edmund Scientific Co., 101 East Gloucester Pike, Barrington, NJ 08007-1380. (609)547-8880. Supplies dinosaur replicas from Carnegie and London Museums of Natural History and wooden dinosaur skeleton models to assemble.

Genesis, Inc., P.O. Box 2242 Mount Vernon, WA 98273 (800) 4PELLET. Sells owl pellets individually or in bulk. Also offers the videotape "Ecology and the Barn Owl."

National Science Teachers Association (NSTA) (800)722-NSTA. Supplies fossil activity kit and teacher's guide on Investigating Science with Dinosaurs. Request a free catalog.

U.S. Department of the Interior, Earth Science Information Centers, 507 National Center, Reston, VA 22092. (800)USA-MAPS. Supplies U.S. Geological surveys map products and earth science publications.

Ward's Natural Science Establishment, Inc., P.O. Box 92912, Rochester, NY 14692-9012 (800)962-2660. Supplies various science materials, including mineral and fossil specimens.

Answer Key

Is This a Dinosaur? (pages 4–5)

Dinosaurs: (B) *Deinonychus*, (H) *Triceratops*, (I) *Stegosaurus*, (L) *Apatosaurus*, (M) *Ankylosaurus*

Non-Dinosaurs: (A) *Elasmosaurus*, (C) *Smilodon or Saber-toothed Cat*, (D) *Dimetrodon*, (E) *Archelon*, (F) *Ichthyosaur*, (G) *Crocodile*, (K) *Pteranodon*, (N) *Woolly Mammoth*

Possible Dinosaur: (J) *Archaeopteryx* is sometimes referred to as a feathered dinosaur because its hands, hips, legs, and skull were very like those of small theropods.

Future Fossil Hunt (page 10)

Students need to use reference books to find what types of fossils are found today. Among these are footprints; feather, leaf, and skin imprints; imprints; skeletons; feces; teeth; and insects trapped in amber which was once tree sap.

The list of possible future fossils should include fallen leaves, feathers, dead plants and animals, and other items which would last through millions of years. Man-made items such as candy wrappers or pieces of clothing would not fossilize.

Interpreting Earth's Time Line (page 20)

1. It took about a billion years before life forms appeared on Earth.
2. These were single celled algae and bacteria.
3. Corals, bivalves, trilobites, and jawless armored fish first appeared during the Ordovician Period. Primitive algae and seaweeds, jellyfish, sponges, starfish, and worms lived in the Cambrian Period.
4. Plants were needed to provide oxygen for the atmosphere on Earth.
5. Amphibians are animals which lay their eggs in water, live in the water as young, then develop the capacity to live on the land. An example of this is the frog.
6. Humans have only been on earth for about 2 million years.
7. Scientists think the dinosaur era was ended by an asteroid or comet striking Earth and clouding the atmosphere with dust. This would cut down on the amount of sunlight that could reach the surface. Therefore, temperatures would drop and many plants would die, thus affecting the plant-eaters and meat-eaters. A recent theory is that this impact may also have set off devastating volcanic action in other parts of the planet (see Resources article of Leon Jaroff, "A Double Whammy?")
8. See time line for details.

Where Are Dinosaur Fossils Found? (page 22)

The author could find no reference to a Dinodontosaurus. Most likely this is an imaginary dinosaur included with the real ones.